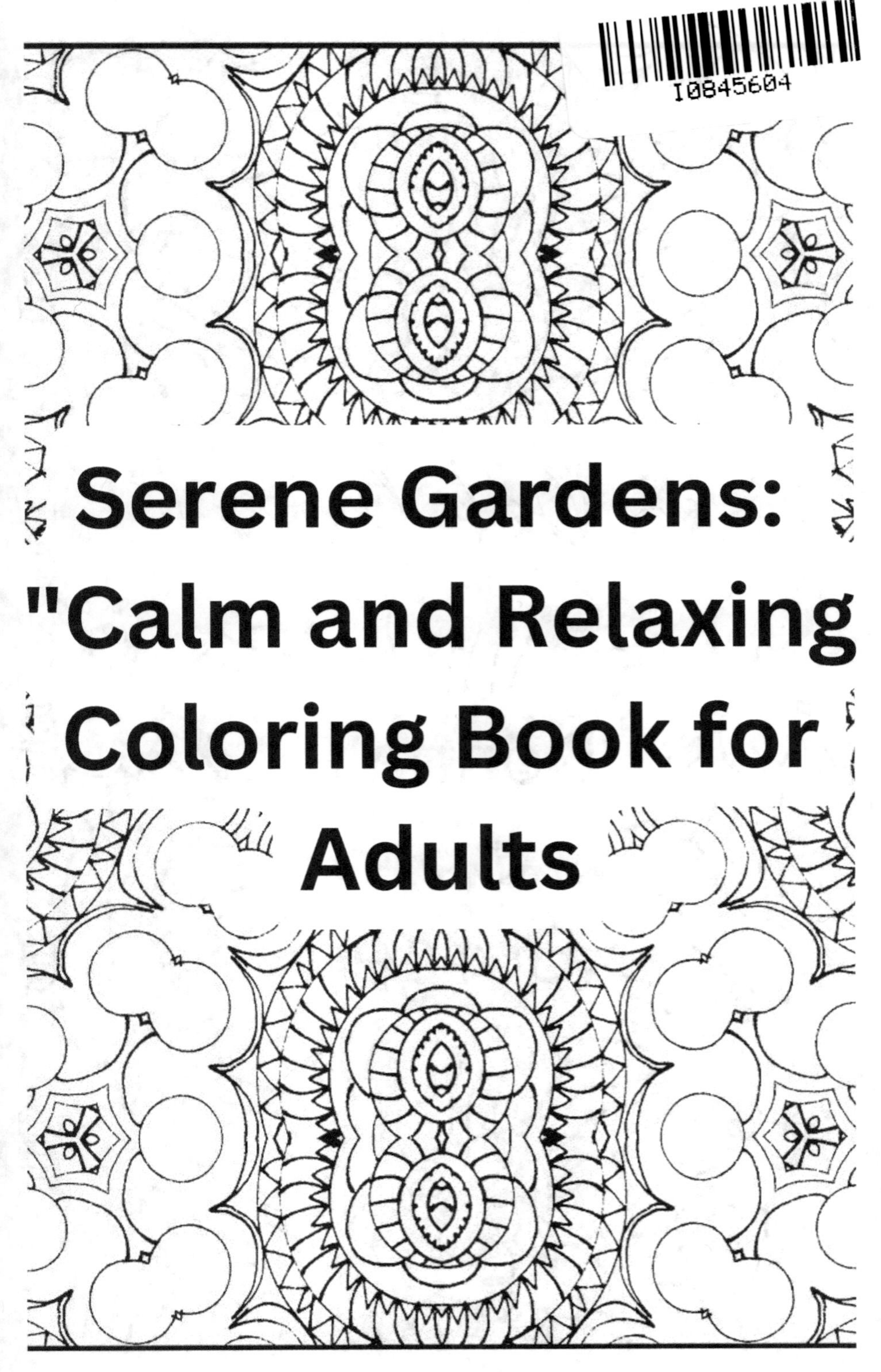

Serene Gardens: "Calm and Relaxing Coloring Book for Adults

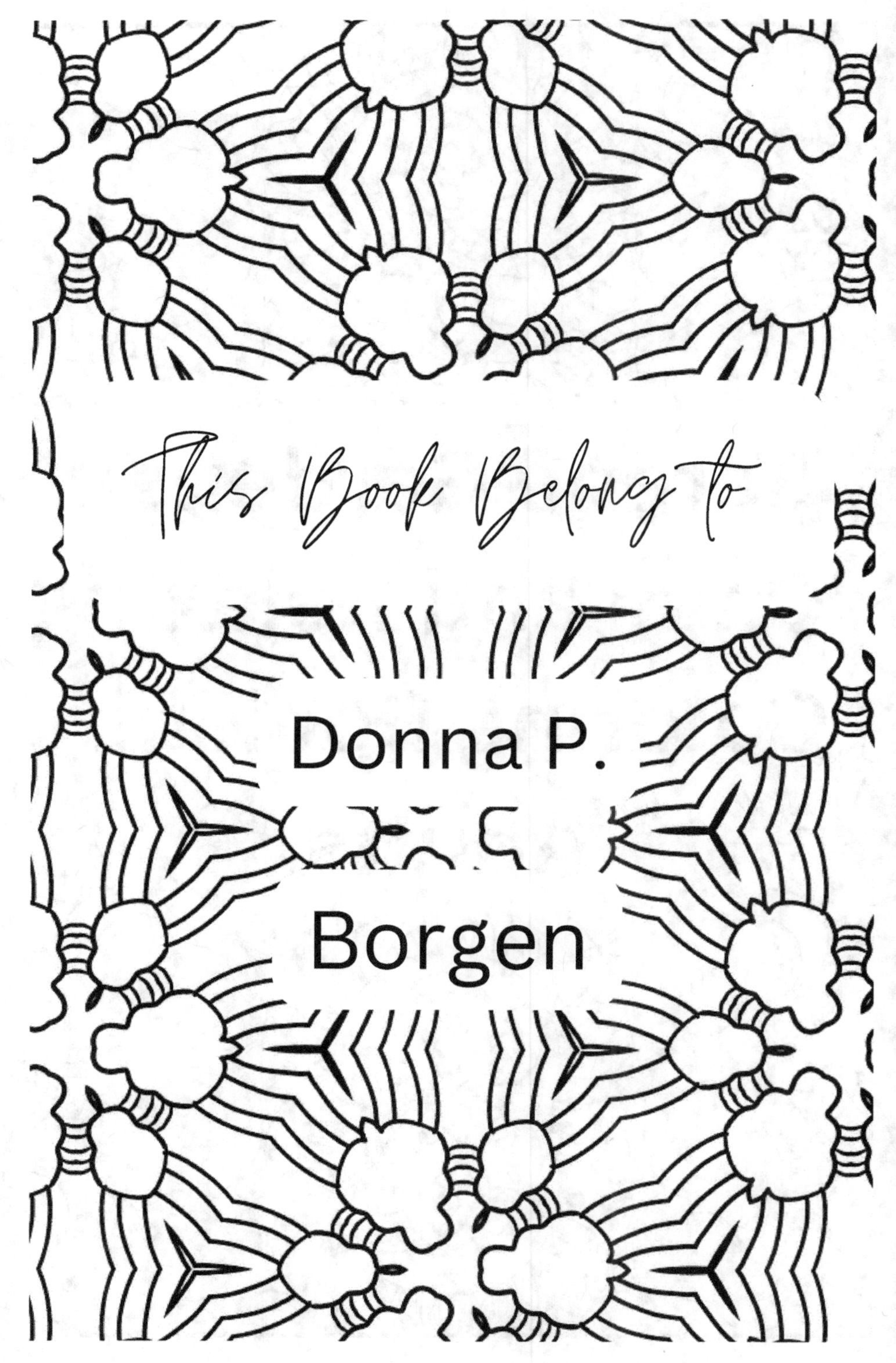
This Book Belong to
Donna P.
Borgen

How to Use this Book

Paint Your World this coloring book, you can explore and unwind. It's your platform; therefore, there are no restrictions or pressure.
Create Your Style: Choose from a variety of pencils, markers, and crayons. It's your creativity.
Moments of Mindfulness: With each stroke, seek tranquility. Take it easy and enjoy yourself.
Personal touch: Draw inspiration from life or let your imagination run wild.
Share Your Work: Are you proud of your work? Share it with your friends on social media. Simple framing: Our pages are easily removed for display or gifting.
Accept Creativity: Get fully involved, relish the process, and produce your masterpiece. Have fun coloring!

Test your Color Here

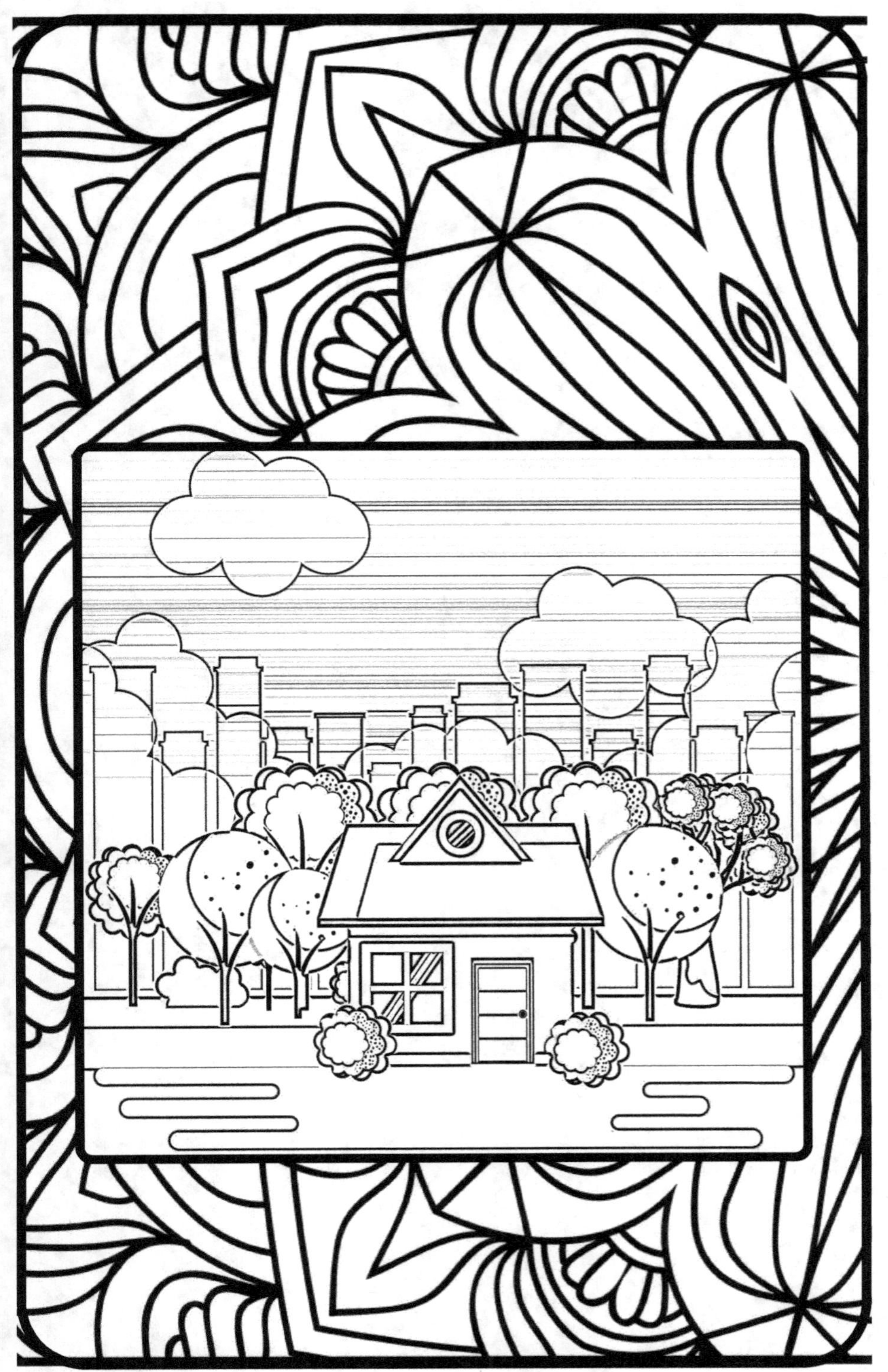

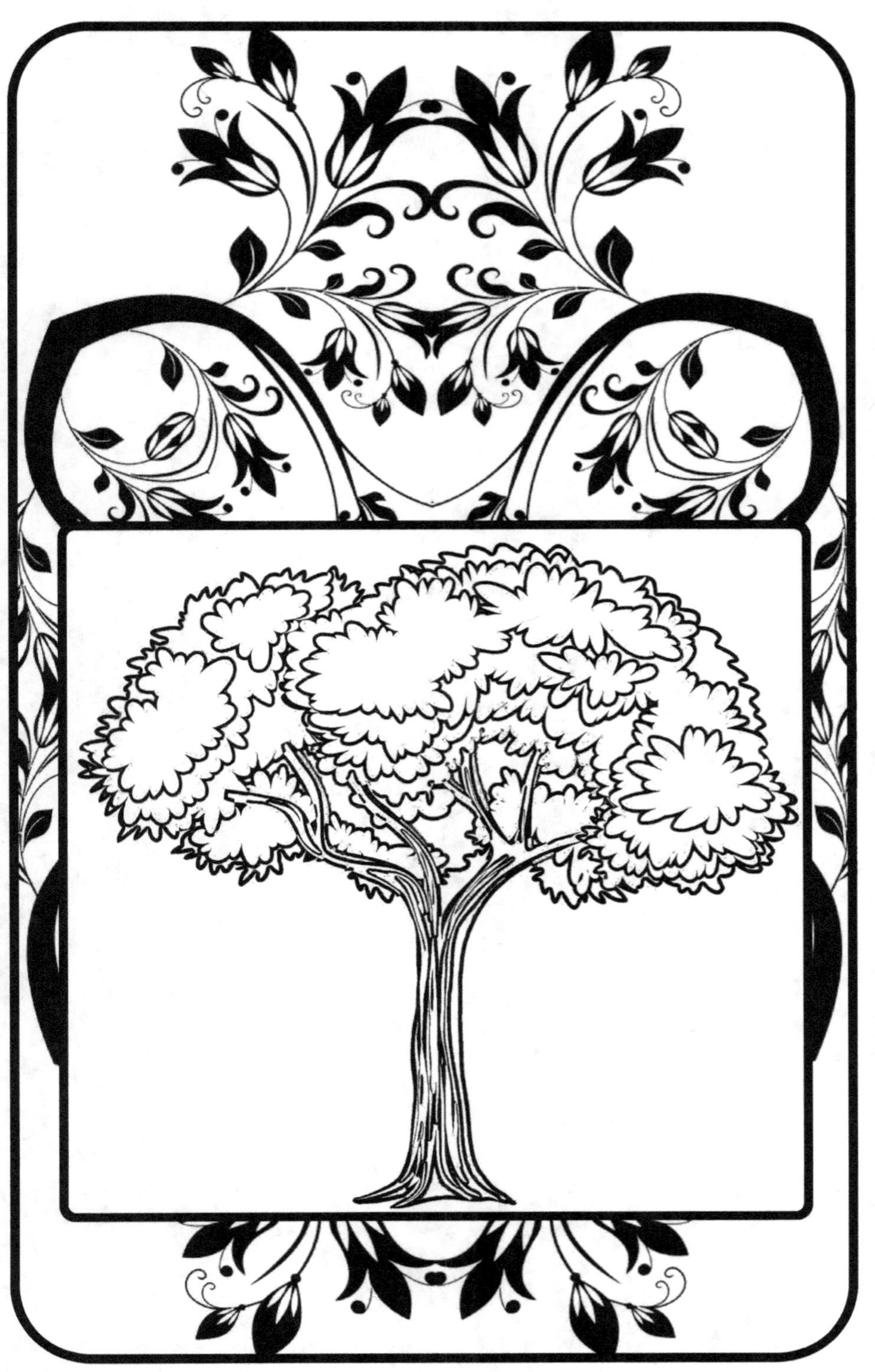

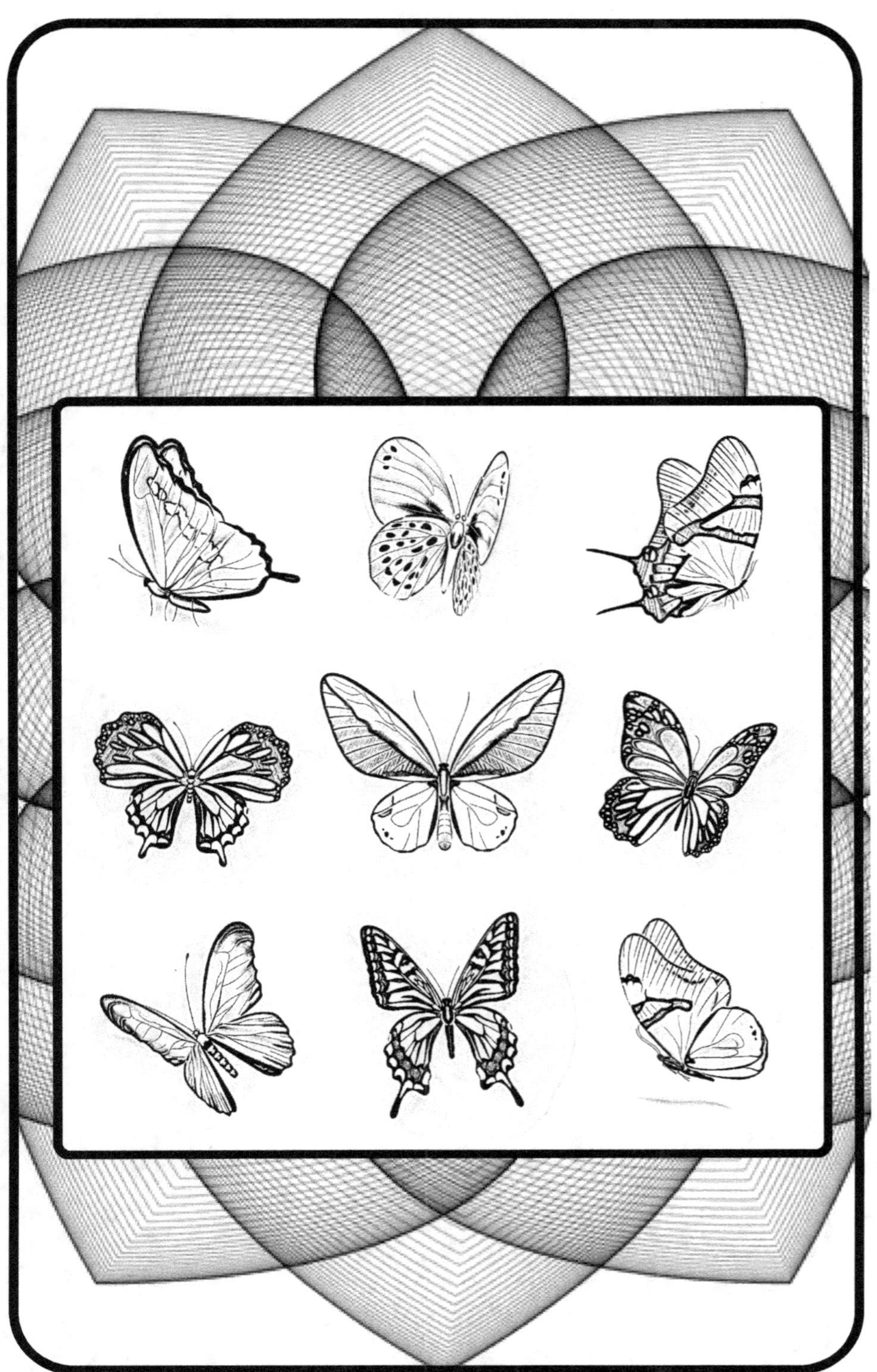

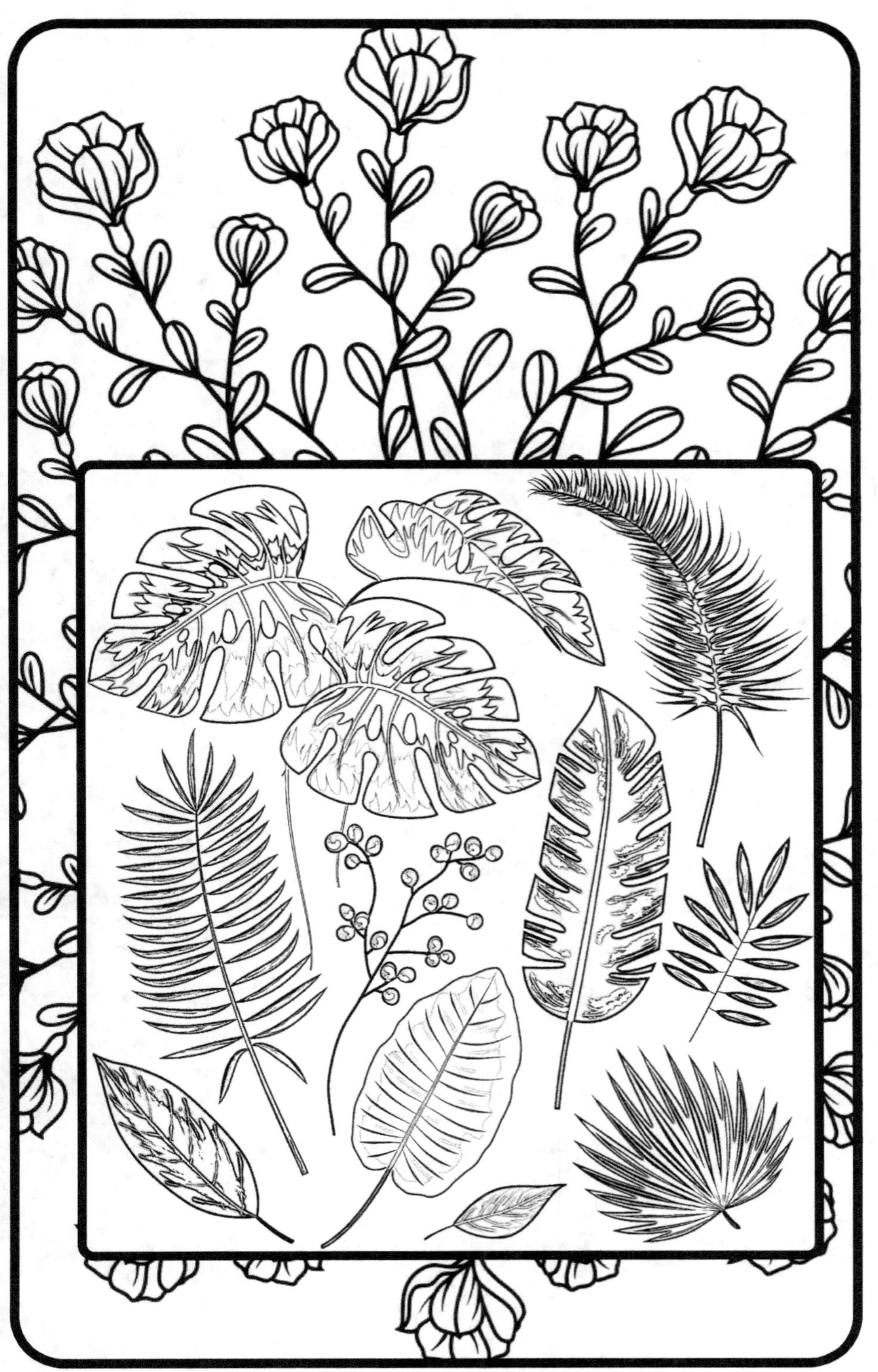

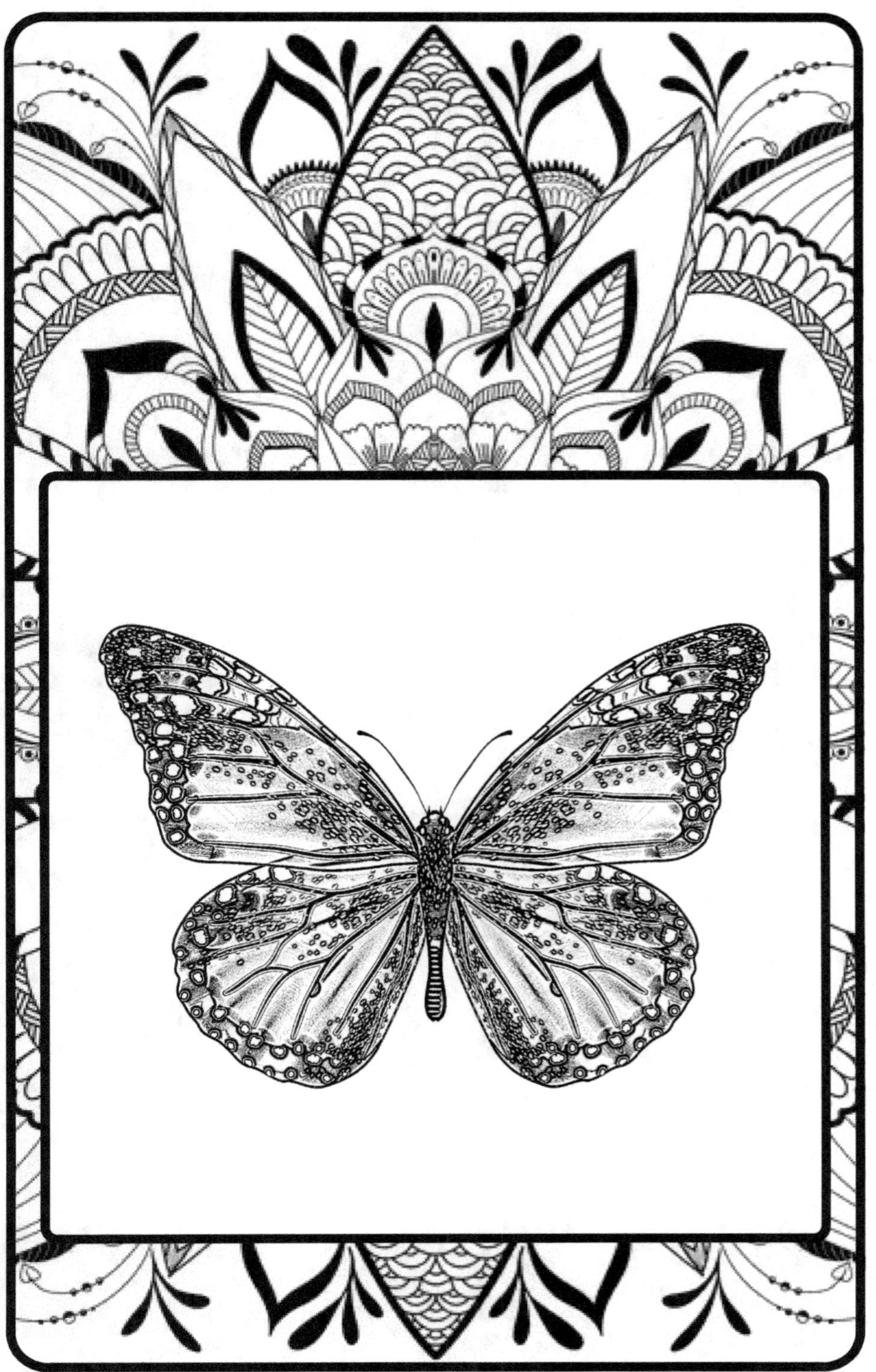

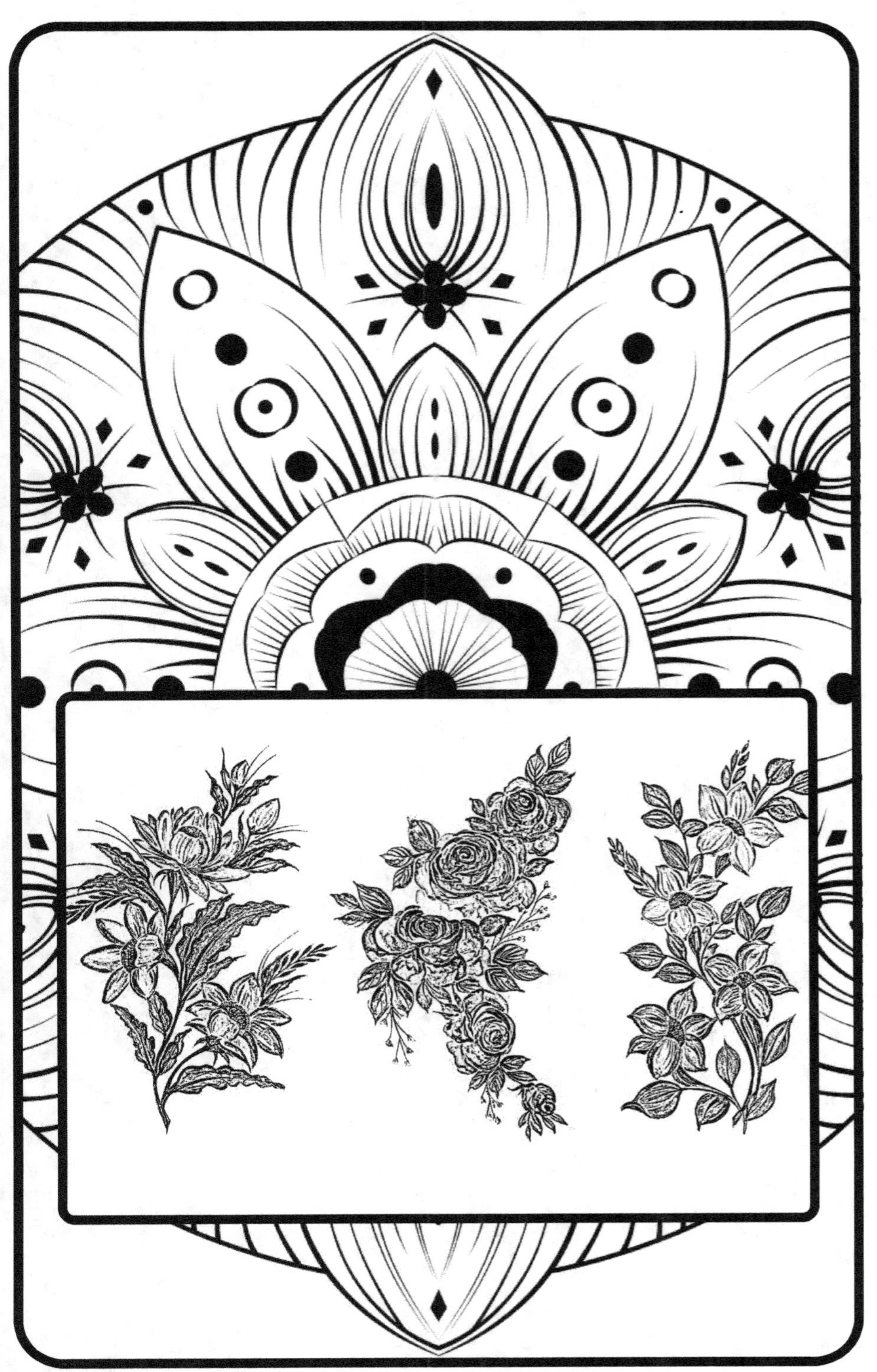

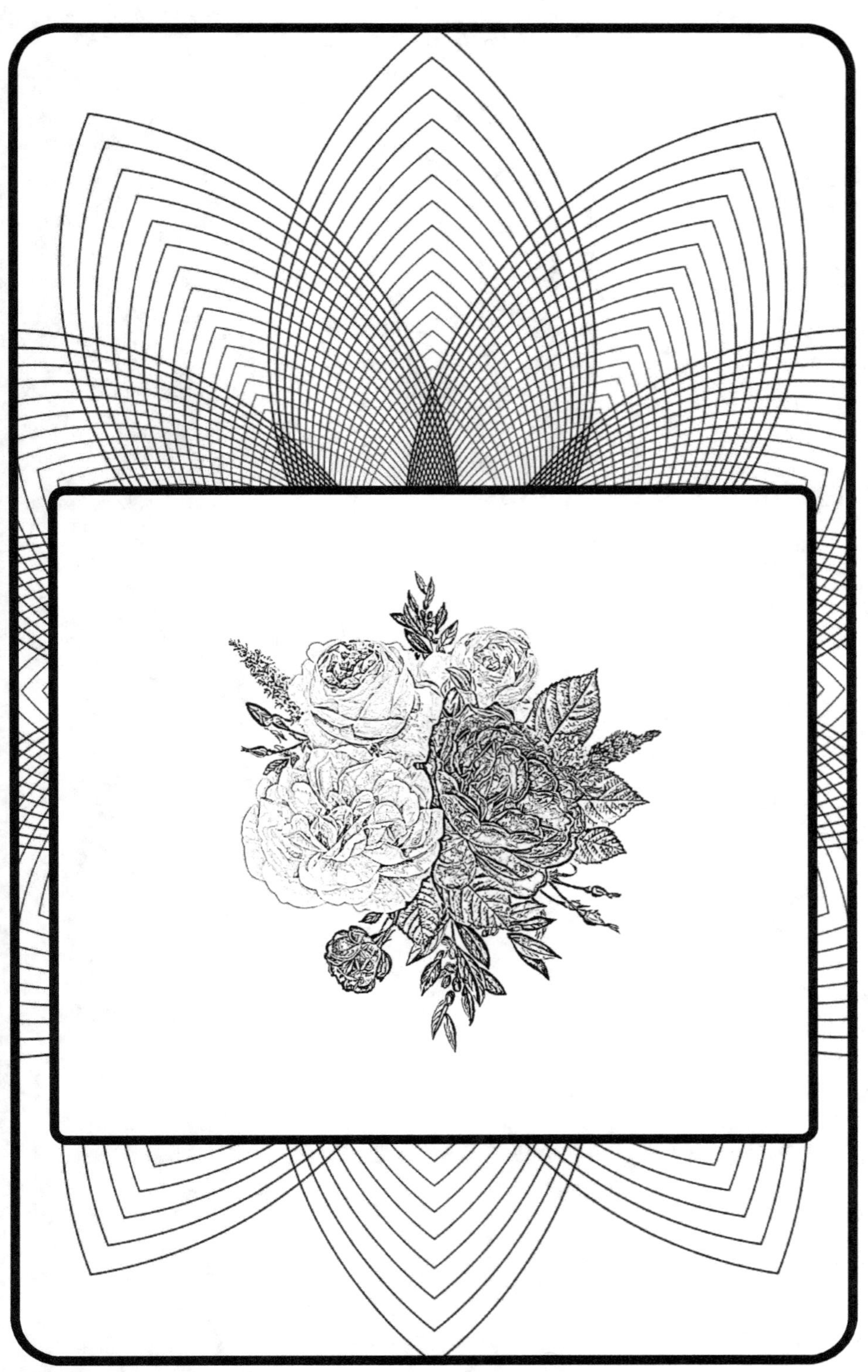

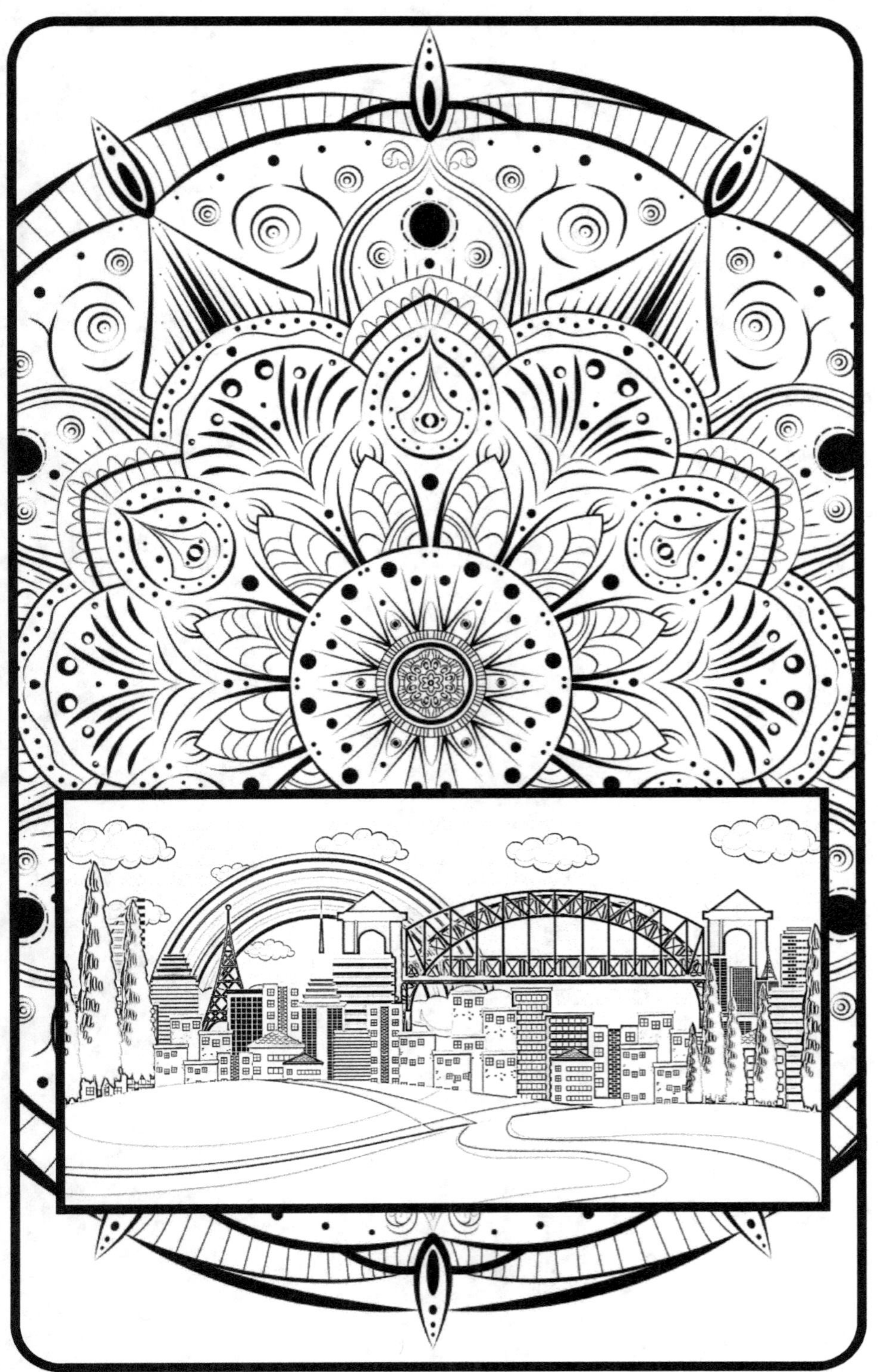

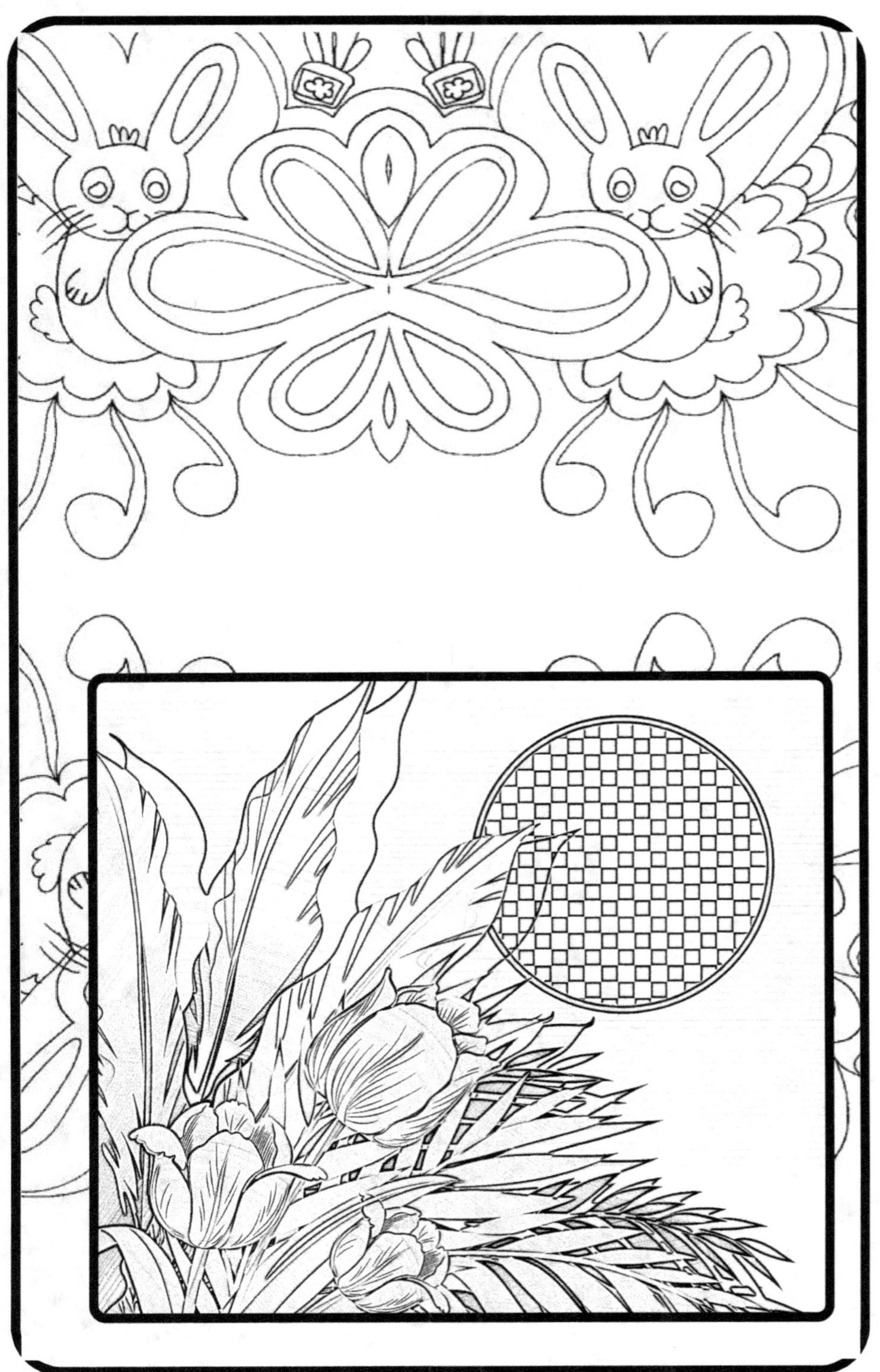

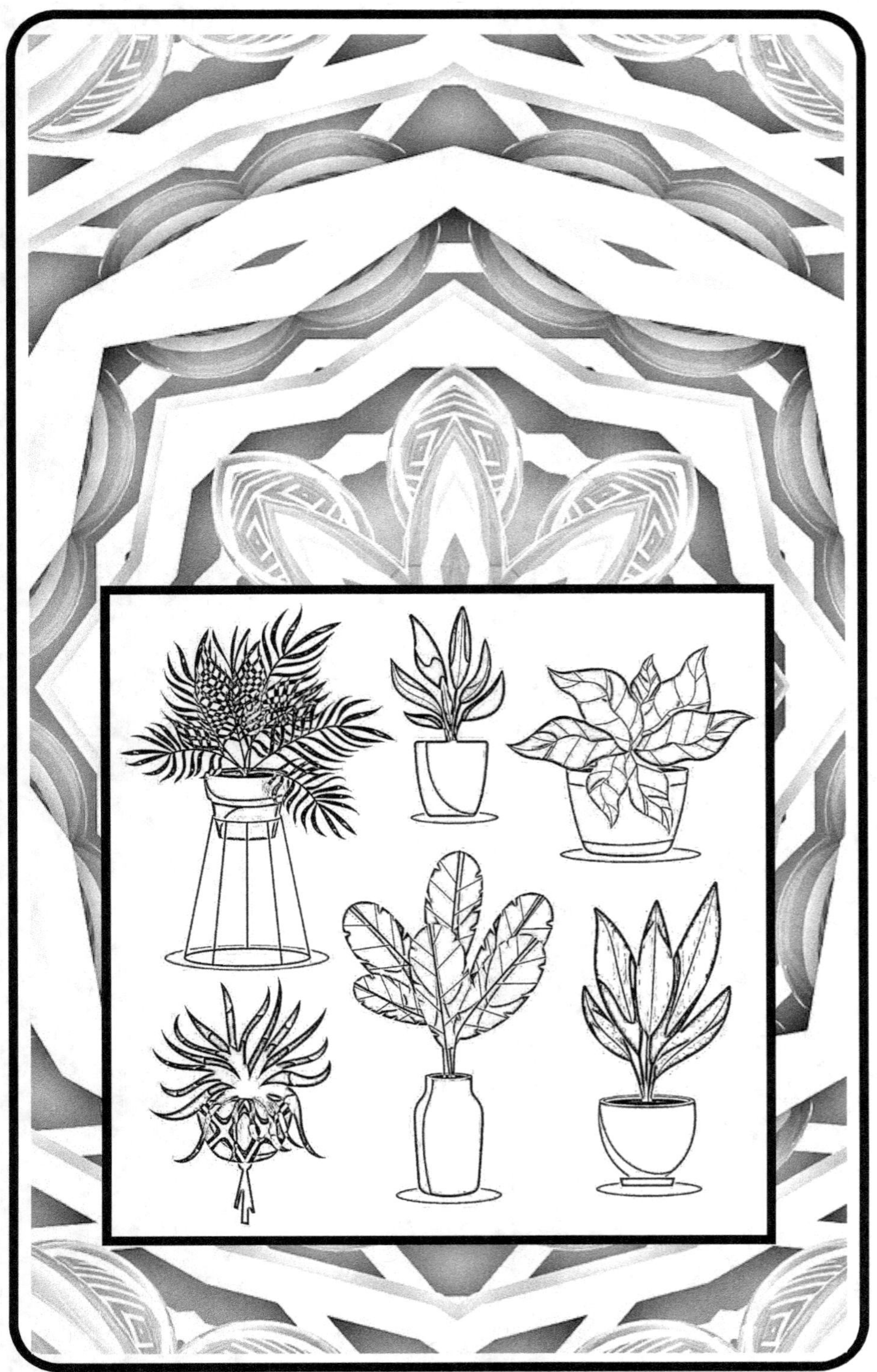

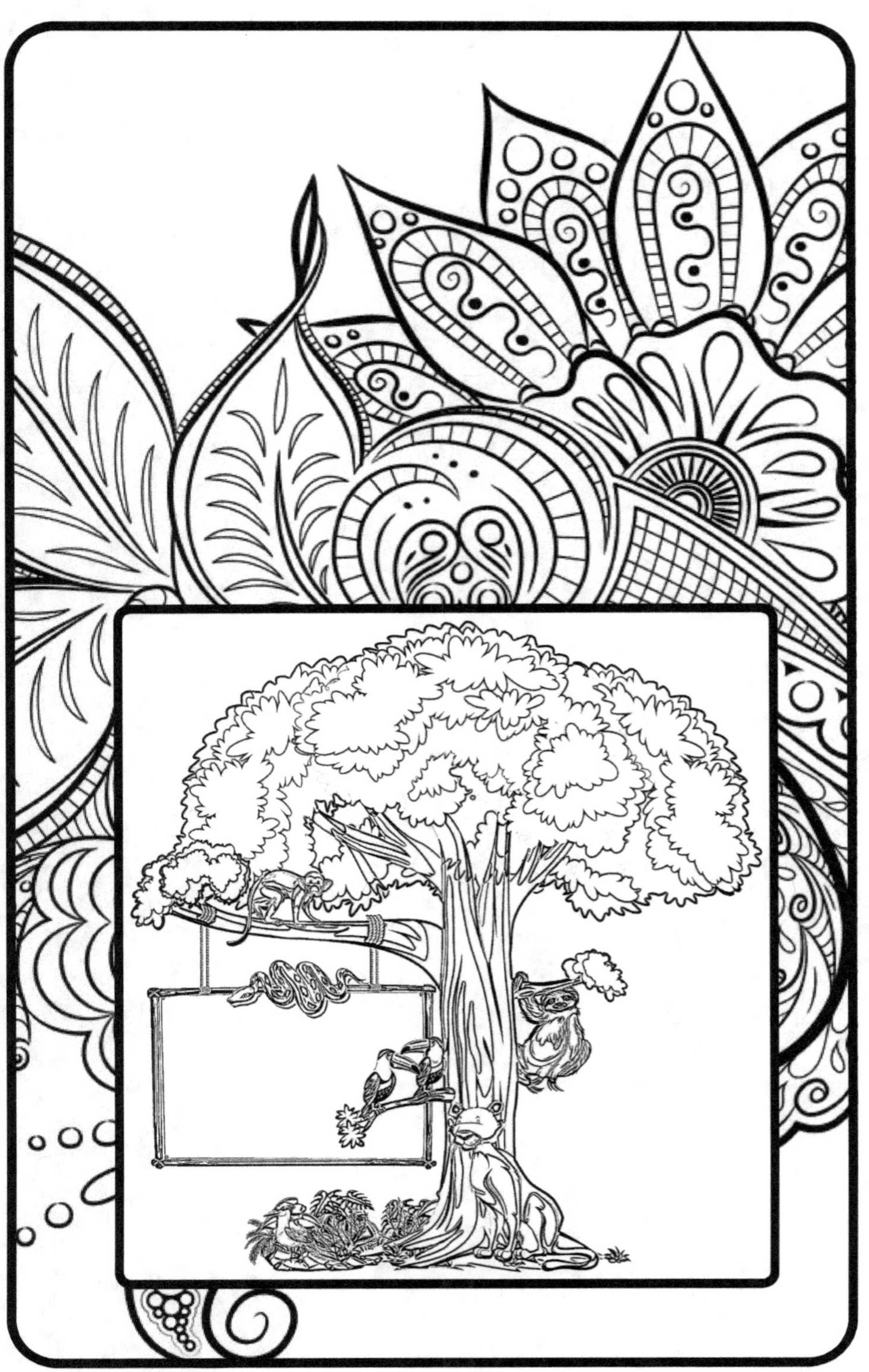

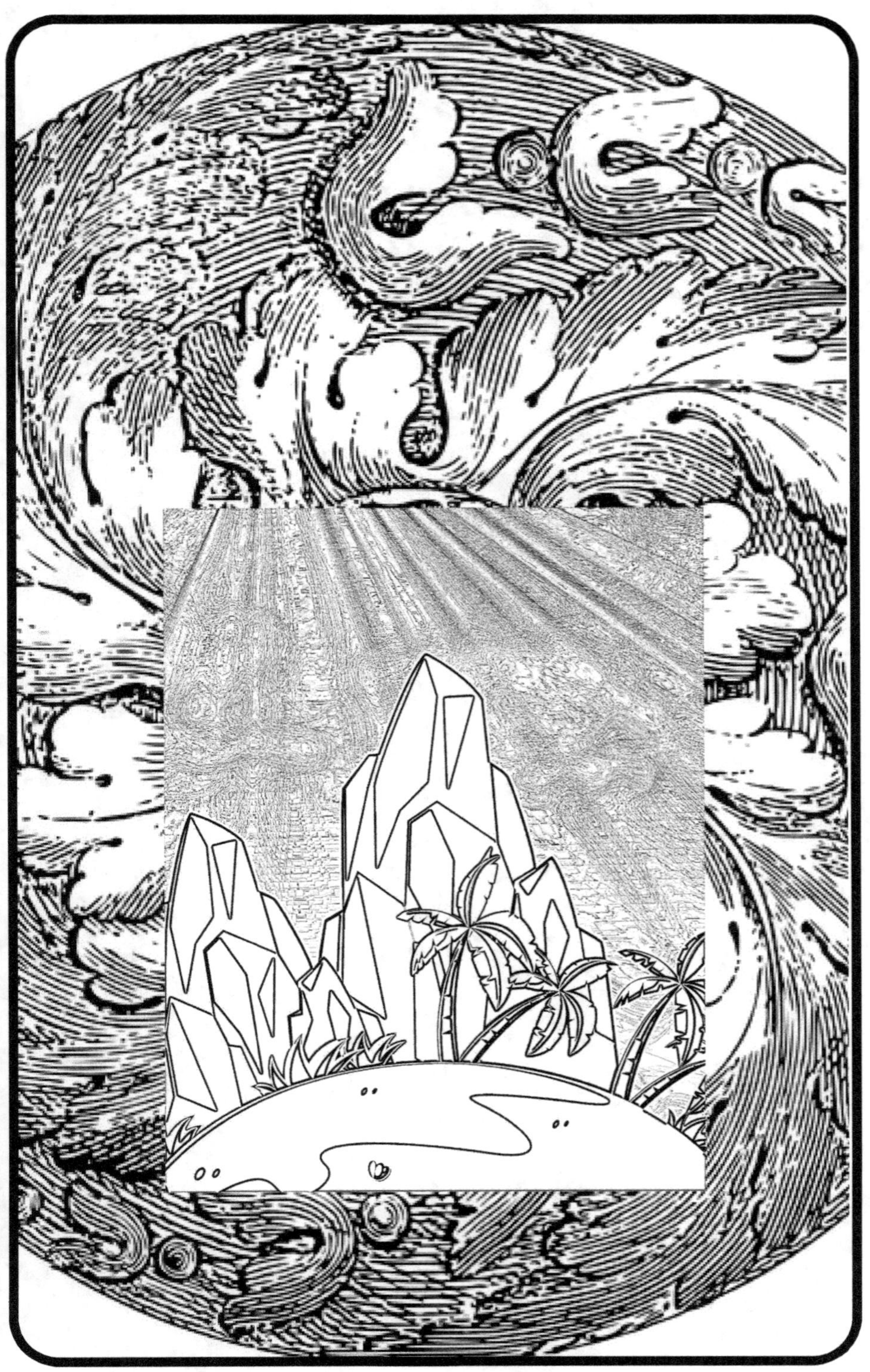

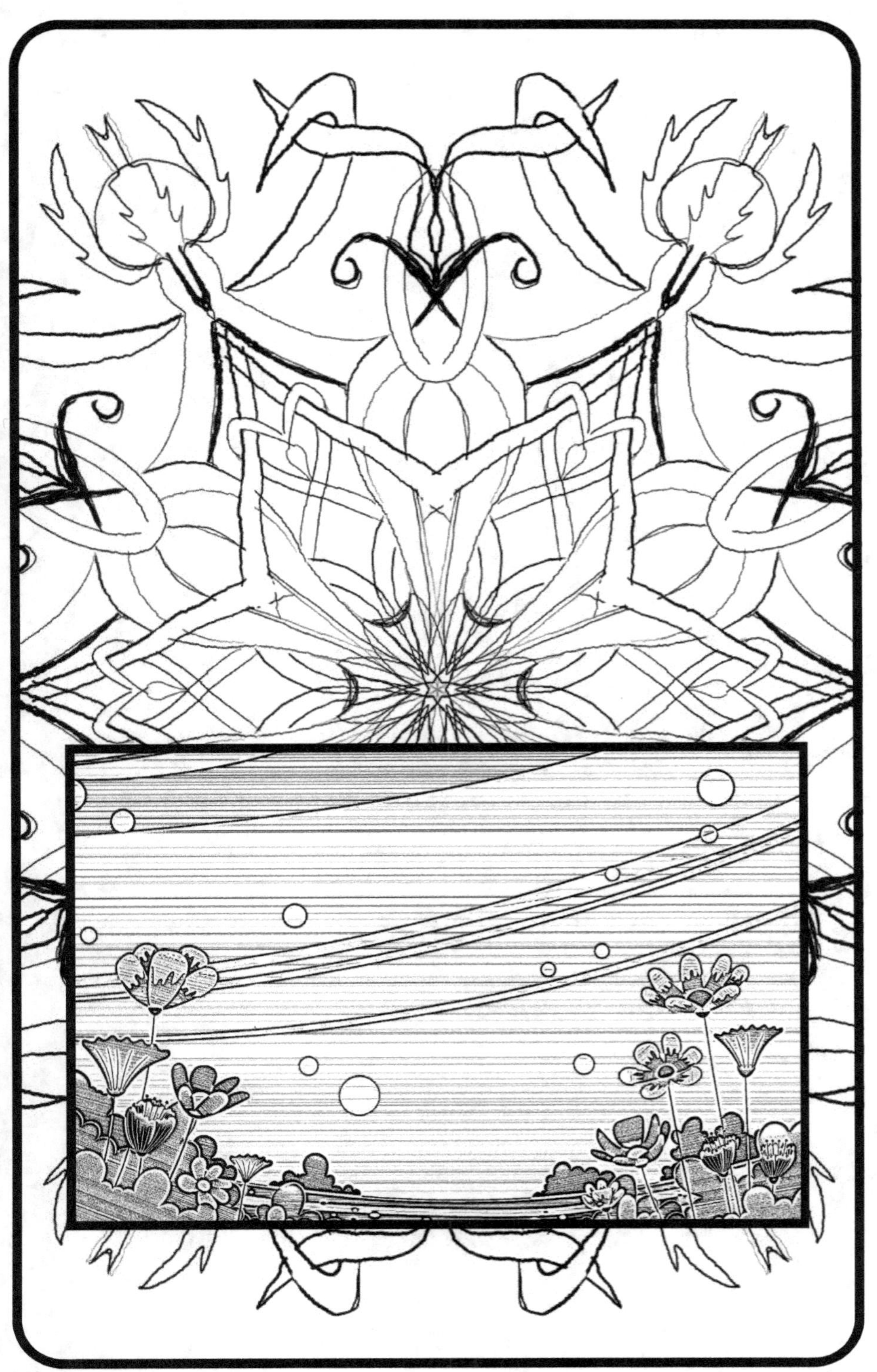

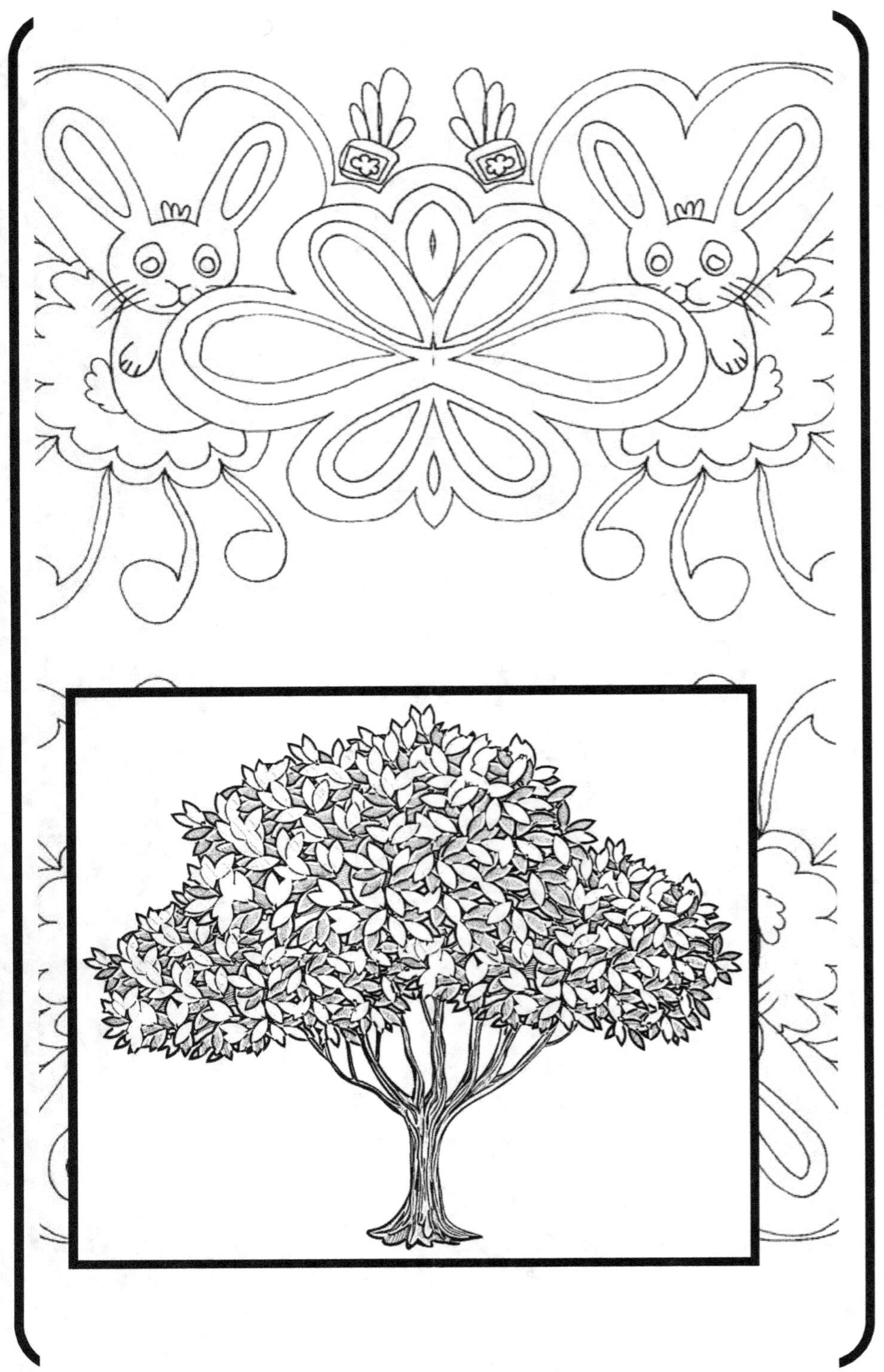

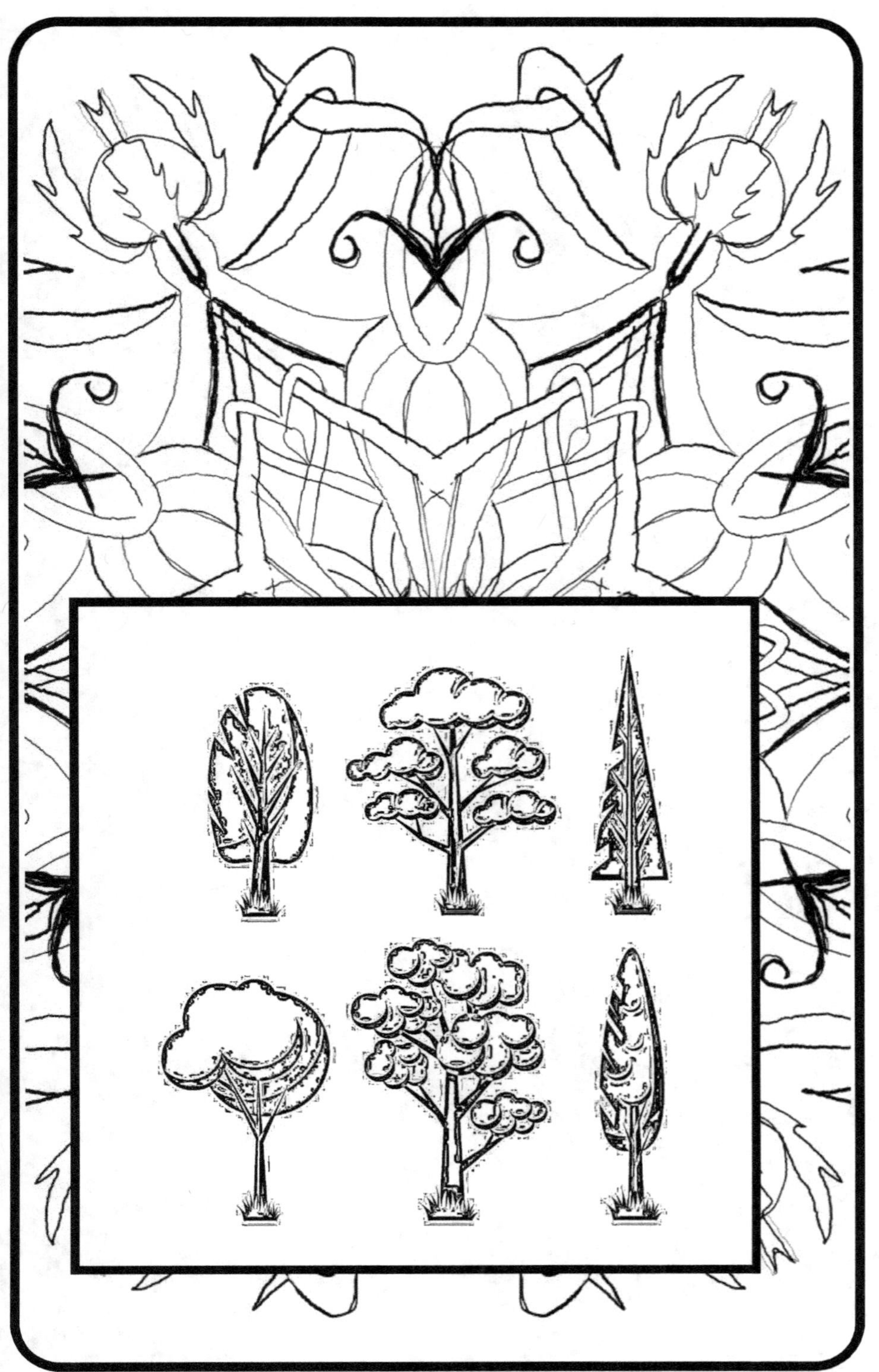

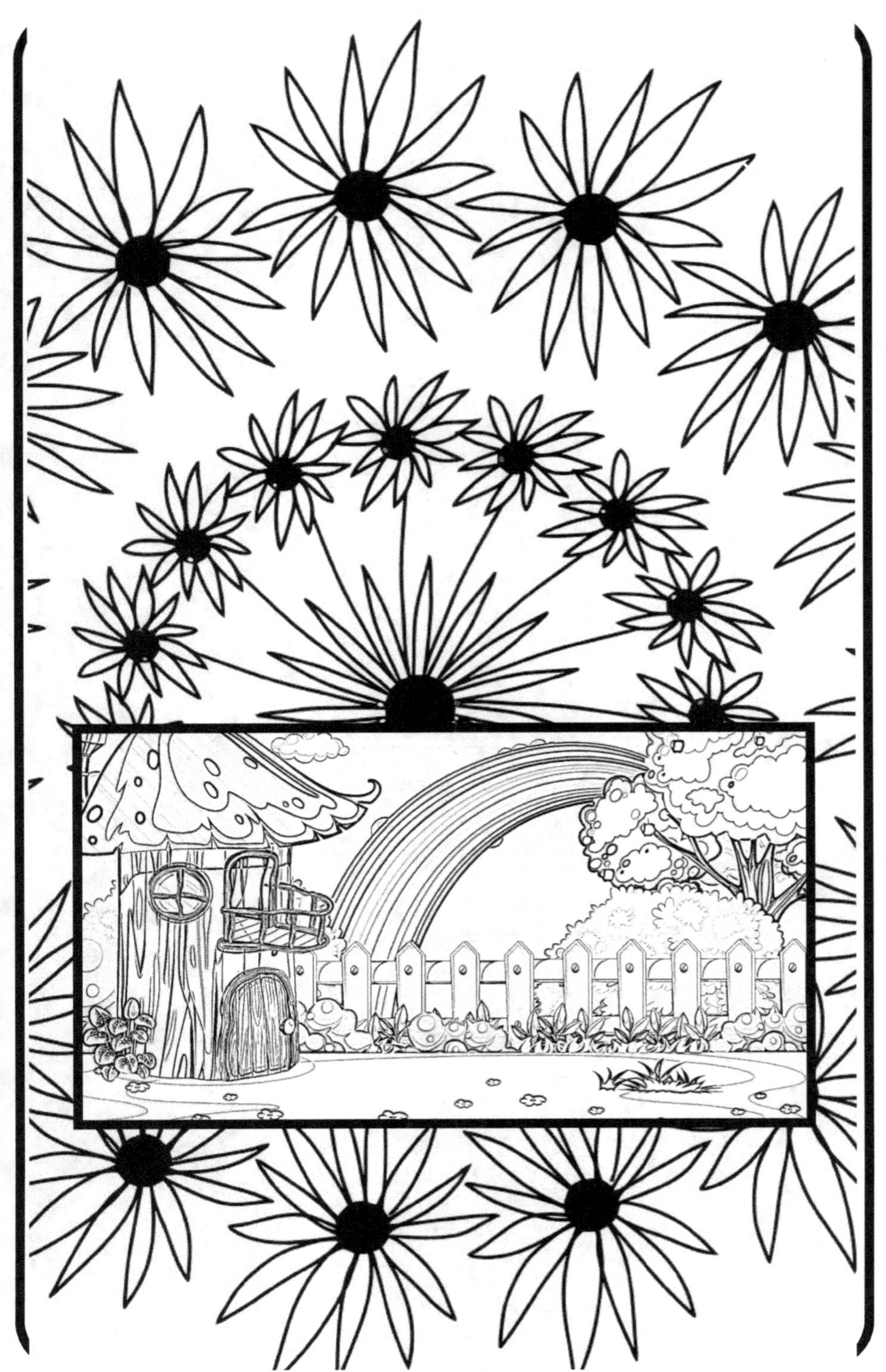

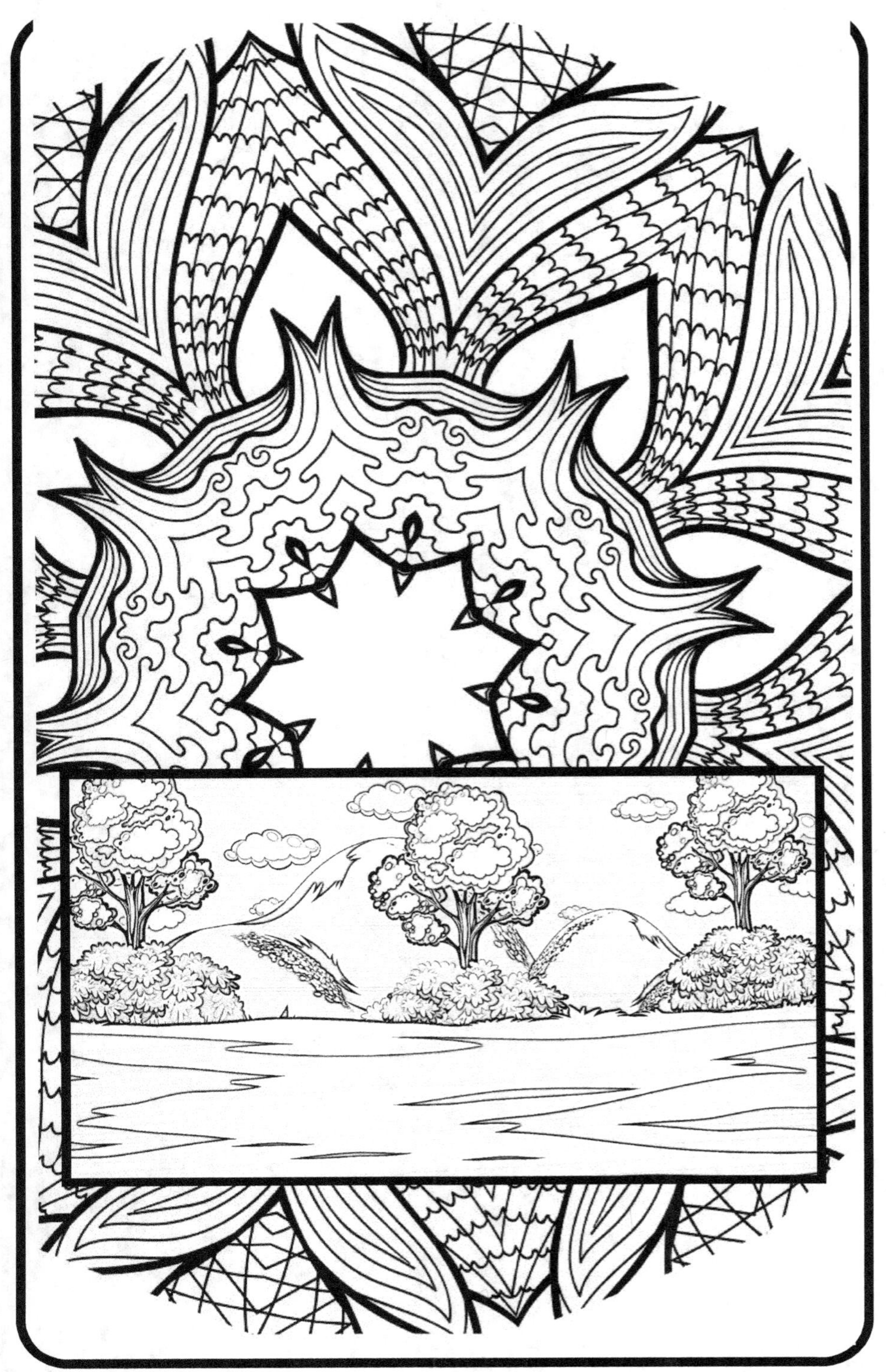

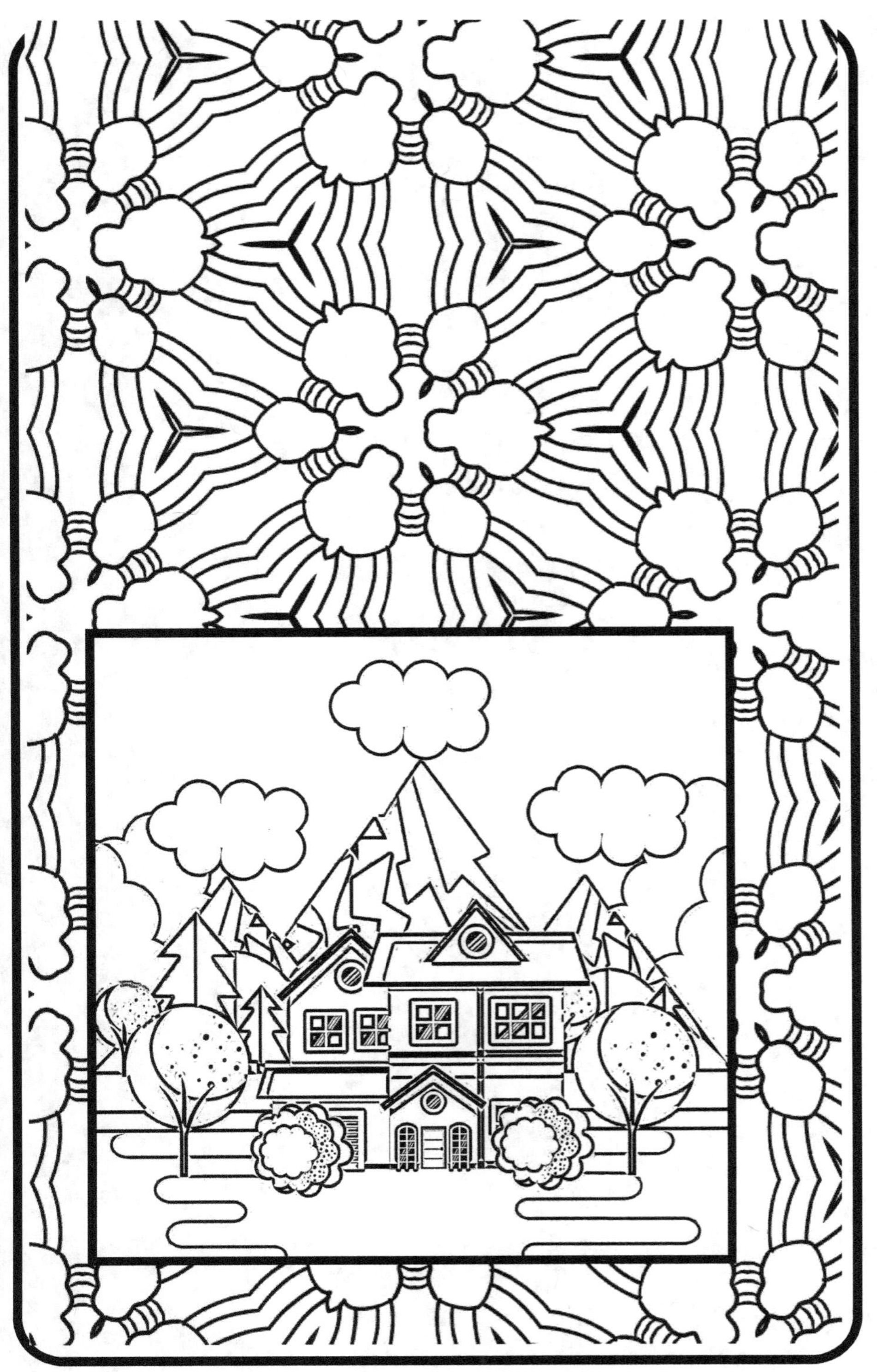

Summary

Greetings from the colorful, imaginative, and expressive realm of self-expression. This book functions as your blank canvas, haven, and leisure area. Here, you can express your feelings and ideas through painting. Inhale deeply, select your colors and allow your artistic journey to begin. Savor the trip, let your imagination run wild, and have a blast. Your creativity, individuality, and self-expression are all reflected in this book. Enjoy your coloring!

www.ingramcontent.com/pod-product-compliance
Lightning Source LLC
Chambersburg PA
CBHW071034260726
48661CB00007B/3020